INSIDE THE
NFL

D0851427

PITTSBURGH
STEELERS

BY WILLIAM MEIER

SportsZone

An Imprint of Abdo Publishing
abdobooks.com

abdobooks.com

Published by Abdo Publishing, a division of ABDO, PO Box 398166, Minneapolis, Minnesota 55439. Copyright © 2020 by Abdo Consulting Group, Inc. International copyrights reserved in all countries. No part of this book may be reproduced in any form without written permission from the publisher. SportsZone™ is a trademark and logo of Abdo Publishing.

Printed in the United States of America, North Mankato, Minnesota
042019
092019

Cover Photo: Joe Sargent/Getty Images Sport/Getty Images
Interior Photos: Gene J. Puskar/AP Images, 4–5; John Bazemore/AP Images, 6; Mark J. Terrill/AP Images, 8; Walter Stein/AP Images, 11; Nate Fine/NFL/Getty Images Sport/ Getty Images, 13; NFL Photos/AP Images, 17; Harry Cabluck/AP Images, 19; Tony Tomsic/ AP Images, 21, 22, 43; Walter Iooss Jr./Sports Illustrated/Set Number: X23075 TK1 F20/ Getty Images, 25; Vernon Biever/AP Images, 26; Heinz Kluetmeier/Sports Illustrated/ SetNumber: X24133/Getty Images, 28; Michael Conroy/AP Images, 30-31; Tony Dejak/ AP Images, 35; G. Norman Lowrance/AP Images, 36; Paul Spinelli/AP Images, 38; Keith Srakocic/AP Images, 40

Editor: Patrick Donnelly
Series Designer: Craig Hinton

Library of Congress Control Number: 2018966050

Publisher's Cataloging-in-Publication Data

Names: Meier, William, author.
Title: Pittsburgh Steelers / by William Meier
Description: Minneapolis, Minnesota: Abdo Publishing, 2020 | Series: Inside the NFL | Includes
        online resources and index.
Identifiers: ISBN 9781532118623 (lib. bdg.) | ISBN 9781532172809 (ebook) | ISBN
        9781644941157 (pbk.)
Subjects: LCSH: Pittsburgh Steelers (Football team)--Juvenile literature. | National Football
        League--Juvenile literature. | Football teams--Juvenile literature. | American football--
        Juvenile literature.
Classification: DDC 796.33264--dc23

TABLE OF
CONTENTS

CHAPTER 1

A SIXTH RING

When the Pittsburgh Steelers hire a head coach, they really commit to him. When Mike Tomlin was hired in 2007, he was only the third Steelers head coach since 1969. And the ones who came before him were legends. Chuck Noll won four Super Bowls. Bill Cowher won one. They were the two winningest coaches in team history.

Cowher retired at the end of the 2006 season, just a year removed from winning the franchise's fifth Super Bowl. Expectations for the team were still high. They always were among Steelers fans.

The Steelers were known for tough defense throughout their history. And Tomlin had been the defensive coordinator for the Minnesota Vikings in 2006, when his group

Mike Tomlin brought enthusiasm and intensity to the Steelers' sideline when he was hired as head coach in 2007.

James Harrison, *center*, sheds the last two Cardinals tacklers at the 3-yard line before completing his 100-yard interception return for a touchdown.

surrendered the fewest rushing yards in the National Football League (NFL). It was a great fit.

The 2007 Steelers allowed the second-fewest points and the fewest yards in the NFL. They went 10–6 but lost in the first round of the playoffs. In 2008 they allowed both the fewest points and fewest yards. They went 12–4, won their division again, and were Super Bowl favorites. Pittsburgh then defeated the San Diego Chargers 35–24 and the Baltimore Ravens 23–14 to reach Super Bowl XLIII against the Arizona Cardinals.

Thanks to some big plays from their strong defense, the Steelers built an early lead. Included in that was a play that will forever live among the top highlights in Super Bowl history. Trailing 10–7 late in the first half, the Cardinals had the ball on the Steelers' 1-yard line and were threatening to take the lead.

Cardinals quarterback Kurt Warner dropped back to pass. Steelers linebacker James Harrison stepped in front of the intended receiver at the goal line and made the interception. He then rumbled down the sideline 100 yards for a touchdown. Instead of falling behind, the Steelers were up 17–7.

But the Cardinals' passing combination of Warner and Larry Fitzgerald threatened to ruin the Super Bowl for the Steelers. Fitzgerald caught a 1-yard touchdown early in the fourth quarter to make it a 20–14 game. A safety gave the Cardinals two points and the ball with less than three minutes to play. Then Warner's 64-yard touchdown throw to Fitzgerald with 2:37 left gave Arizona a 23–20 lead.

But the Steelers had an impressive quarterback and receiver duo of their own in Ben Roethlisberger and Santonio Holmes. When Pittsburgh won the Super Bowl three years earlier, Roethlisberger had been a second-year quarterback who relied primarily on his teammates to carry the offense.

The Steelers' Santonio Holmes makes what proved to be a game-winning touchdown catch in Super Bowl XLIII.

But in Super Bowl XLIII, he was a key player. He answered Fitzgerald's touchdown by completing five of seven passes on the next drive.

When Holmes caught a pass and raced 40 yards to the Arizona 6-yard line, the Steelers were no longer just looking for a field goal to force overtime. Then, on the game's key play, Roethlisberger scrambled and lofted a pass to the corner of the end zone.

Holmes leaped high. He caught the ball, but his body was leaning out of bounds. He stretched to get his toes in bounds, barely tapping the turf for a 6-yard touchdown with 35 seconds left. Pittsburgh held on to win 27–23.

The Steelers' defense had a tough day with Warner and Fitzgerald. But defensive end LaMarr Woodley sacked Warner near midfield in the closing seconds, forcing a fumble that Pittsburgh recovered. At age 36, Tomlin became the youngest head coach to win a Super Bowl in the game's history. And the Steelers became the first team to win the Super Bowl six times.

SUPER MVPS

Santonio Holmes followed in the footsteps of some great Steelers wide receivers when he was named Super Bowl Most Valuable Player (MVP). Lynn Swann caught four passes for 161 yards in Super Bowl X to win MVP. Thirty years later, Hines Ward won the trophy after catching five passes for 123 yards and a touchdown. Holmes caught nine passes for 131 yards and the game-winning touchdown in his MVP effort against Arizona.

CHAPTER 2

THE EARLY YEARS

Art Rooney, a resident of the North Side of Pittsburgh, enjoyed success in sports early in the 1900s. Rooney won a number of national boxing titles and was named to the US Olympic team, though he never did fight in the Olympic Games. He played minor league baseball from 1920 to 1925. An arm injury stopped him short of making it to the big leagues.

Rooney kept active in sports by playing semipro football for many teams around the Pittsburgh area. In the 1930s, the difference between a semipro football team and an NFL team was not nearly as large as it is now. Rooney moved from playing football to running his own team when he founded an NFL team for Pittsburgh on July 8, 1933.

Art Rooney, left, and NFL commissioner Bert Bell discuss the NFL Draft in 1947.

SUPREME SIGNING

Art Rooney signed University of Colorado All-American Byron "Whizzer" White to a $15,800 contract in 1938. It was the largest in the NFL at the time. Rooney was trying to turn around his Pittsburgh football team, but it didn't quite work out. White led the NFL in rushing in 1938. It was his only year with the Pirates. White led the league in rushing two out of three years in the league, including in 1940 with the Detroit Lions. He went on to greater fame after his football career. White served as a US Supreme Court Justice for 31 years until he retired in 1993.

As was common at the time, the football team took the name of the city's baseball team. Rooney's team was originally called the Pirates.

The Pirates struggled in the early years. They ran through five coaches in seven years and won just 22 games out of 80 played in that span. The team was based at Forbes Field in Pittsburgh. It did not draw many fans. Rooney moved some home games to Johnstown, Pennsylvania, and Latrobe, Pennsylvania, as well as Youngstown, Ohio, and even New Orleans.

The team was renamed the Steelers in 1940. This was in recognition of the steel industry's importance in Pittsburgh.

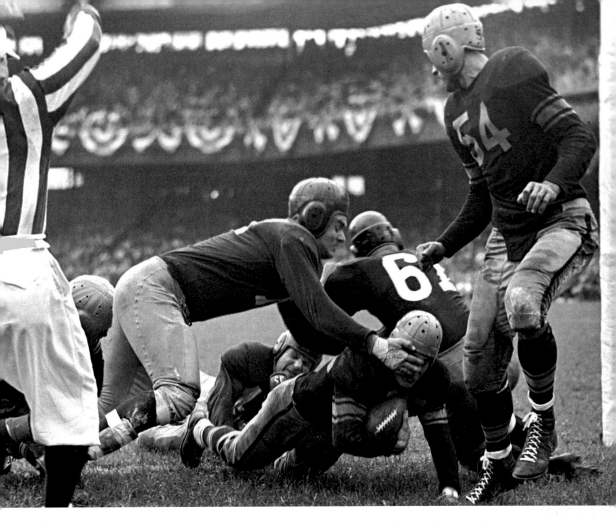

Bill Dudley, *bottom*, scores a touchdown for the Steelers in a 1946 game at Washington. He made the Pro Football Hall of Fame in 1966.

But the new name didn't change their fortunes. The team won only three games total in its first two years under the name Steelers. After nine years, the team had suffered eight losing seasons.

Head coach Walt Kiesling led a turnaround in 1942. The Steelers improved from 1–9–1 the year before to 7–4 and

TEMPORARY MERGERS

Many of the young men who played in the NFL were called to duty in World War II. Rosters and available talent were depleted by 1942.

In 1943 the Philadelphia Eagles and Pittsburgh Steelers made the decision that they could not field teams on their own. They agreed to play the season as the Phil-Pitt Steagles. They shared coaches and players and split time between the two cities. The cooperation worked well enough for the Pennsylvania teams to combine for a 5–4–1 record.

In 1944 the Eagles were ready to go back on their own. The Steelers decided to combine with the Chicago Cardinals. The second arrangement did not work nearly as well. The Chi/Pitt Cards/Steelers did not win a game. They went 0–10. The combined team scored more than seven points just three times while losing by 21 or more in seven of their 10 games.

second place in the Eastern Division. After losing their first two games, the Steelers won seven out of the next eight. Bill Dudley led the NFL in rushing. He also led the Steelers in passing. Dudley and lineman Chuck Cherundolo were All-Pro players who helped the defense pick up three shutouts. The NFL, however, changed during the World War II years. Many players left the NFL to join the military. The Steelers could not keep their momentum because they did not have their own team for two seasons. They instead joined with other teams to form combined squads.

The first 39 seasons in Steelers history included just one playoff team—the 1947 Steelers. Pittsburgh was rolling at 7–2 that season after a 24–7 victory over the New York Giants. After getting blown out by the Chicago Bears, the Steelers gave up the Eastern Division lead to Philadelphia when the Eagles beat them 21–0. However, the Steelers finished with a 17–7 victory over the Boston Yanks to tie the Eagles for first place at 8–4. The tie set up a playoff for the East title. The Eagles again blanked the Steelers 21–0 to end Pittsburgh's season.

The Steelers then went from 1950 to 1971 with just four winning seasons and no playoff berths. The team hit its low point in 1969, the first season under coach Chuck Noll. It was a franchise-worst 1–13.

The next year, the American Football League (AFL) merged with the NFL. The Steelers were one of three NFL teams to join the 10 AFL teams to form the American Football Conference (AFC). Pittsburgh, the Baltimore Colts, and Cleveland Browns were put with the AFL newcomers. It wasn't the only big change in store for the Steelers. As the new decade began, they were about to become the team of the 1970s.

CHAPTER 3

BECOMING IMMACULATE

The Steelers had spent nearly 40 years as one of the NFL's least successful teams. In 1972 they began a journey toward a remarkable level of success. That year the Steelers jumped to the top of the AFC Central Division. They went 11–3 for the second-best record in the conference and in the NFL.

On December 23, 1972, Pittsburgh was in position for its first playoff victory ever. The host Steelers slugged it out with the Oakland Raiders in a scoreless first half. Pittsburgh then held the lead for much of the second half. But then Oakland quarterback Ken Stabler ran 30 yards for a touchdown to give the Raiders a 7–6 lead with 1:13 remaining.

Lynn Swann makes an acrobatic catch against the Cowboys in the Super Bowl.

FRANCO HARRIS

The Steelers took running back Franco Harris with the thirteenth overall pick of the 1972 NFL Draft. He was a key member of their four Super Bowl championship seasons in the 1970s. Harris played 12 seasons with the Steelers and one with the Seattle Seahawks. When he retired, Harris ranked third in NFL history in rushing yards (12,120). Harris was chosen as the MVP of Pittsburgh's first Super Bowl win. It was a 16–6 victory over Minnesota in Super Bowl IX in January 1975. He rushed for 158 yards.

Harris teamed with Rocky Bleier in the Steelers' backfield from 1972 to 1980. In 1976, both rushed for more than 1,000 yards.

Pittsburgh's comeback hopes looked faint at best. The Steelers faced fourth-and-10 at their 40-yard line with 22 seconds left. Quarterback Terry Bradshaw threw deep for running back Frenchy Fuqua near Oakland's 35. Bradshaw's pass arrived the same time as Oakland safety Jack Tatum. Fuqua and Tatum collided violently. The ball bounced backward, looping high in the air. Steelers running back Franco Harris caught it just before it hit the ground at Oakland's 42. He cut toward the sideline and began a footrace to the end zone.

Many players on the Steelers' sideline were running and following Harris when he made it to the end zone with five

After "the Immaculate Reception," Franco Harris runs past a Raider to score in the 1972 playoff game.

seconds left. The touchdown gave Pittsburgh a 13–7 victory. It was the Steelers' first playoff win in team history. The play became known as "the Immaculate Reception."

A week later, Pittsburgh lost to the unbeaten Miami Dolphins in the AFC Championship Game. The Steelers led twice, including once in the second half, before losing 21–17. Pittsburgh was arguably the NFL's second-best team to Miami in 1972. The Steelers might not have won the ultimate prize yet. But things were clearly changing in Pittsburgh.

CHUCK NOLL

Through 2018 Chuck Noll was one of just two coaches in NFL history to win four or more Super Bowls. Noll had been a defensive assistant with the Los Angeles/San Diego Chargers and the Baltimore Colts before he became Pittsburgh's coach. His first Steelers team finished 1–13 in 1969. Noll then helped build Pittsburgh into the team of the 1970s with its amazing success in the NFL Draft. Noll posted winning marks in 15 of his final 20 seasons.

The 1973 Steelers went to the playoffs as a wild card and lost big to the Raiders in Oakland in the first round. The 1974 Steelers started a streak of six straight division titles. They then beat the Buffalo Bills 32–14 in a divisional playoff game and earned another rematch with the Raiders. This time Pittsburgh defeated host Oakland 24–13 in the AFC title game.

Defense was on display in the Steelers' first Super Bowl season. NFL Defensive Player of the Year "Mean" Joe Greene was joined by Defensive Rookie of the Year Jack Lambert on a unit that held six opponents to seven points or fewer. The Raiders managed just 29 rushing yards in the AFC Championship Game. The Vikings had only 17 in the Super Bowl.

The only scoring in the first half of Super Bowl IX came when defensive end Dwight White tackled Vikings quarterback Fran Tarkenton in the end zone for a safety and a 2–0 lead.

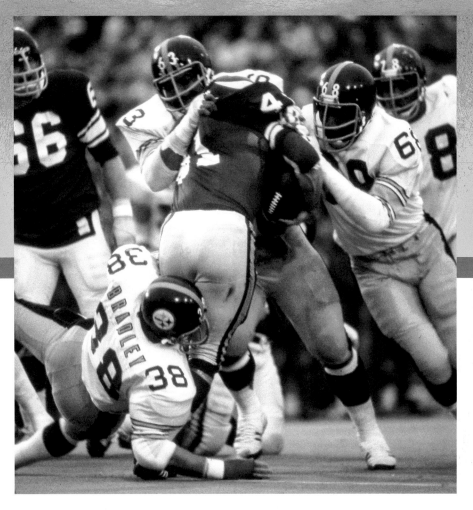

The Steel Curtain defense stuffed running back Dave Osborn (41) and the Minnesota Vikings in Pittsburgh's Super Bowl victory in January 1975.

The Steelers went on to win 16–6. Harris had 34 carries for 158 yards and a touchdown.

In 1975 the Steelers won 11 consecutive regular-season games and finished 12–2. Including the playoffs, they held 10 opponents to 10 points or fewer. The Steelers stopped the

Steelers safety Mike Wagner lays a huge hit on Dallas quarterback Roger Staubach.

Baltimore Colts 28–10 and once again knocked off Oakland 16–10 in the playoffs on the way to Super Bowl X against the Dallas Cowboys.

Steelers wide receiver Lynn Swann put together an MVP performance in the Super Bowl with four catches for 161 yards. He beat Dallas' defense deep for his last reception. Bradshaw stood in to take a hit that knocked him out of the game. He launched a long pass on third-and-four that Swann grabbed and took into the end zone for a 64-yard touchdown. The Steelers led 21–10 with 3:02 left.

But Cowboys star quarterback Roger Staubach was not about to give up. He quickly drove the Cowboys down the field and threw a touchdown pass with 1:48 remaining. But the Steelers held on to win 21–17.

The "Steel Curtain" defense had roughed up Staubach and sacked him seven times. Swann, meanwhile, thrilled the crowd with a record-setting performance. It earned him MVP honors for the game. After decades of disappointment, the Steelers were back-to-back Super Bowl champions.

STEEL CURTAIN

The Steelers of the 1970s put together many of the game's top players of that time. Their physical, intimidating defense became known as the "Steel Curtain." It featured four future Hall of Famers. Those players were tackle "Mean" Joe Greene, linebackers Jack Lambert and Jack Ham, and cornerback Mel Blount. Other stars of the defense included tackle Ernie Holmes and ends L. C. Greenwood and Dwight White.

CHAPTER 4

TEAM OF
THE DECADE

By the late 1970s, Pittsburgh had built a roster filled with talent that was unmatched in the NFL. The Steelers won four Super Bowls in a six-season period. Through 2018, they are still the only team to accomplish that in league history.

After their first two titles, the Steelers suffered a two-year lull—at least by their lofty standards. Pittsburgh fell 24–7 to Oakland in the AFC Championship Game after an injury-hampered 1976 season. The Steelers then lost 34–21 to the Denver Broncos in the first round of the 1977 playoffs.

But Pittsburgh was back in form in 1978, posting the NFL's top record in the newly expanded 16-game schedule by going 14–2. Then the Steelers rolled into the Super Bowl

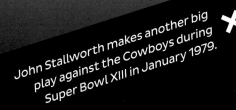

John Stallworth makes another big play against the Cowboys during Super Bowl XIII in January 1979.

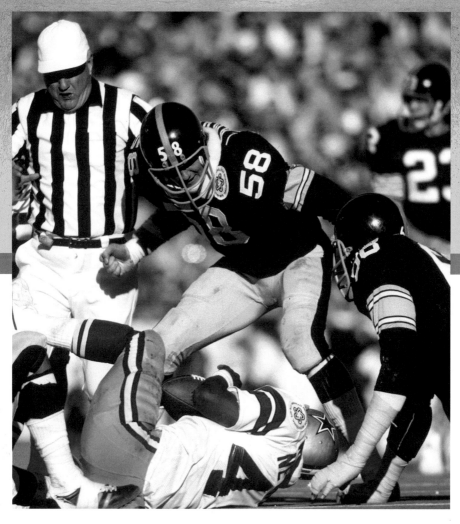

with playoff wins over Denver (33–10) and the Houston Oilers (34–5).

Terry Bradshaw passed for a then-record four touchdowns as Pittsburgh beat Dallas 35–31 in Super Bowl XIII in January

1979. Pittsburgh broke open the game with two touchdowns in 19 seconds midway through the fourth quarter. Franco Harris ran 22 yards for a score. Then Dennis Winston recovered a fumbled kickoff and Bradshaw passed 18 yards to Lynn Swann for a touchdown with 6:51 left, giving them a 35–17 lead. The Cowboys rallied with two late touchdowns, but Rocky Bleier recovered an onside kick with 17 seconds left to clinch the victory.

That made the Steelers the first club to win three Super Bowls. A 12–4 finish in 1979, followed by victories over Miami and Houston in the AFC playoffs, put Pittsburgh in position to set more records.

Pittsburgh faced the Los Angeles Rams in Super Bowl XIV. Bradshaw led the Steelers from behind in the third and fourth quarters for a 31–19 victory. His 47-yard touchdown pass to Swann gave the Steelers a 17–13 lead early in the third quarter. The Rams grabbed the lead right back. But Bradshaw found John Stallworth with a 73-yard touchdown pass early in the fourth quarter to put the Steelers ahead for good. Another Bradshaw-to-Stallworth connection, this one for 45 yards, set up a clinching 1-yard touchdown run by Harris. Despite throwing three interceptions, Bradshaw won his second straight Super Bowl MVP Award.

✖ Terry Bradshaw rolls out to pass against the Rams in Super Bowl XIV.

The victory, which came on January 20, 1980, followed up the 1979 season and officially capped the successful 1970s decade. After winning their first two titles on the strength of their defense, the Pittsburgh offense came through in a big way in the last two. In 1979 the Steelers compiled league-best averages of 391.1 yards and 26.0 points per game. In an

CONSISTENT LINEUPS

The Steelers benefited from consistency throughout their lineup during their dominant run in the 1970s. On defense, left end L. C. Greenwood, left tackle "Mean" Joe Greene, middle linebacker Jack Lambert, and right cornerback Mel Blount each started at the same position for Pittsburgh's four Super Bowl victories in the 1970s. Jack Ham started three of the Super Bowl wins at left linebacker. Defensive backs J. T. Thomas and Mike Wagner also started three of the wins.

The offense also had a number of fixtures in the lineup. Quarterback Terry Bradshaw, running backs Franco Harris and Rocky Bleier, left tackle Jon Kolb, and right guard Gerry Mullins each started all four Super Bowl victories. Wide receivers Lynn Swann and John Stallworth started the last three.

interview 20 years later, Bradshaw talked about what it was like to run that offense.

"I don't know if I gave the team confidence," Bradshaw said. "I know they gave me confidence. It was a great feeling, looking around the huddle, knowing that whatever I wanted to do, I had the guys to do it, 'Here, Franco, you run with the ball. Here, Lynn, you catch it. Okay, John, Rocky, it's your turn.' Imagine yourself sitting on top of a great thoroughbred horse. You sit up there and feel the power. That's what it was like, playing quarterback on that team. It was a great ride."

CHAPTER 5

BACK ON TOP

The 1970s ended, and the San Francisco 49ers ruled the 1980s with four Super Bowl championships. Pittsburgh no longer dominated. The Steelers did remain competitive, though. They hung around .500 for much of the next decade.

Most of the 1970s legends had retired by 1984. But not John Stallworth, who had a career-high 1,395 yards and won NFL Comeback Player of the Year. The Steelers won the AFC Central, and even knocked out the Denver Broncos in the playoffs. But they fell to Miami in a bid for one more Super Bowl appearance. It took until 1985, when they were 7–9, for the Steelers to fall below .500. It was their first losing season in 14 years.

It also was the start of a four-year absence from the playoffs. The Steelers bottomed out with a 5–11 showing

Steelers coach Bill Cowher holds the Lombardi Trophy after beating Seattle 21–10 in February 2006.

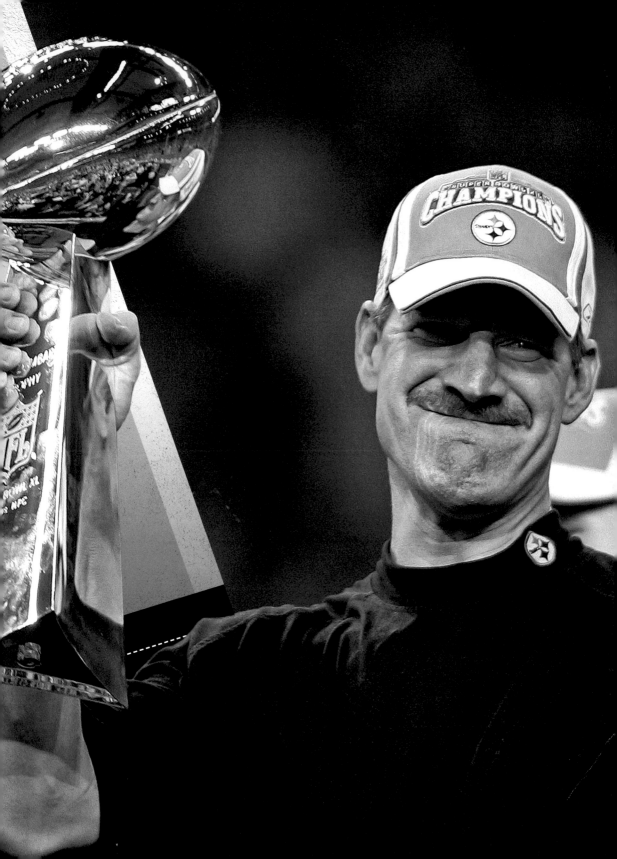

SUPER BOWL DEFEAT

The Steelers were back to being in the playoffs almost every season under coach Bill Cowher. But they had to wait for the ultimate success for an NFL team.

Pittsburgh lost its first home playoff game in 10 years when it fell 24–3 to Super Bowl–bound Buffalo after the 1992 season. The Steelers' first AFC Championship Game at home in 15 years, after the 1994 season, resulted in a 17–13 loss to San Diego.

A year later, the Steelers lost in the Super Bowl for the first time in five tries. Pittsburgh had returned to the Super Bowl with a 20–16 victory over Indianapolis in the AFC title game in January 1996. But the Steelers lost Super Bowl XXX to Dallas, 27–17. Cowboys cornerback Larry Brown set up touchdowns with two second-half interceptions of Neil O'Donnell to give Dallas its fifth Super Bowl title and third in four seasons.

in 1988. The record was Pittsburgh's worst since Chuck Noll's first season as head coach in 1969. The Steelers recovered from a slow start in 1989 to finish 9–7 and make the playoffs as a wild card. But that was the team's final playoff appearance under Noll.

Bill Cowher played linebacker with Cleveland and Philadelphia in the early 1980s. He was the Kansas City Chiefs' defensive coordinator when the Steelers hired him to be their next head coach after Noll retired following the 1991 season.

Pittsburgh returned to being a consistent contender under Cowher. The Steelers returned to the playoffs in his first season. He won NFL Coach of the Year in leading Pittsburgh to an 11–5 record and division title. The Steelers lost in their first playoff game. But they would have many more chances in the coming years.

Pittsburgh won 10 or more games nine times and reached the playoffs 10 times in Cowher's 15 seasons as coach. Cowher's teams, however, were known for their near misses. They lost in the AFC Championship Game four times.

In Cowher's first trip to the conference title game, after the 1994 season, the Steelers were Super Bowl favorites. Tight end Eric Green was even planning his own Super Bowl music video. Instead, the Steelers lost at home to the San Diego Chargers.

Pittsburgh at least made it to the Super Bowl the next year but lost to the Dallas Cowboys. In Cowher's first 13 seasons, the Steelers had a regular season record of 130–77–1. They had won eight division titles. But all they had to show for it was one Super Bowl appearance.

The results of 2004 and 2005 showed that the playoffs truly are a "second season." In 2004, Pittsburgh became the first AFC team ever to go 15–1 in the regular season. But the

DICK LEBEAU

Before he became a legendary coach, Dick LeBeau was a Hall of Fame defensive player with the Detroit Lions. LeBeau played 14 seasons in the NFL. When he retired in 1972, he had the third-most interceptions in NFL history. He got into coaching right away. LeBeau served two stints as Steelers defensive coordinator. Many of the top Steelers defenses in the 1990s and 2000s were led by LeBeau. He created many modern NFL defensive plays such as the zone blitz. LeBeau left the Steelers after the 2014 season. He took a year off and came back to serve as the Tennessee Titans' defensive coordinator. He spent two years in Tennessee before finally retiring at the age of 80 in 2017.

Steelers were unable to get through the conference playoffs. They lost 41–27 to the visiting New England Patriots in the AFC Championship Game. On the other hand, the Steelers were just 7–5 in 2005 before they won their final four games. That earned them the conference's sixth and final playoff berth.

It took the last of those 10 playoff teams under Cowher, in 2005, for the Steelers to return to the top. The Steelers would have to win three road games to reach the Super Bowl. Pittsburgh was up to the challenge. The Steelers became the first team to reach the Super Bowl via that route. They won

Second-year quarterback Ben Roethlisberger helped the 2005 Steelers win the Super Bowl as a wild-card team.

games at Cincinnati (31–17), Indianapolis (21–18), and Denver (34–17) to reach Super Bowl XL in Detroit.

Veteran Steelers running back Jerome "The Bus" Bettis had been uncertain about whether to retire or to return for the

✗ Jerome Bettis runs the ball during Pittsburgh's Super Bowl XL win.

2005 season. The possibility of a Super Bowl in his hometown of Detroit contributed to a decision to come back for one final season. It all worked out perfectly for him. Bettis rushed for 43 yards to help Pittsburgh beat the Seattle Seahawks 21–10.

"It's been an incredible ride," Bettis said. "I'm a champion. I think the Bus' last stop is here in Detroit."

Hines Ward was named MVP of the Super Bowl with five catches for 123 yards. He caught a 43-yard touchdown pass from fellow wide receiver Antwaan Randle El on a trick play in the fourth quarter. Pittsburgh joined San Francisco and Dallas as the only teams to have won five Super Bowls.

Cowher coached one more season, then stepped down. As they had when Noll retired, the Steelers turned to a 34-year-old for his first head coaching assignment. Tomlin, a former standout defensive coordinator with the Minnesota Vikings, took over.

Tomlin led the Steelers to the playoffs in his first season and to a Super Bowl title in his second. That gave Pittsburgh the most Super Bowl titles with six. Tomlin assembled a core of players that kept the Steelers competitive for more than a decade.

Just like Noll had with Terry Bradshaw, Tomlin had a reliable franchise quarterback in Ben Roethlisberger. He was the team's first draft pick in 2004. Roethlisberger was a dual-threat quarterback who could run and pass effectively. He went

Safety Troy Polamalu was a key part of the Steelers' defense from 2003 to 2014.

on to break nearly every Pittsburgh record for quarterbacks, including most passing yards and most passing touchdowns.

Tomlin's Steelers teams also had reliable running backs. First there was Rashard Mendenhall. He rushed for 1,273 yards in 2010 as the Steelers made it to Super Bowl XLV. Then there was Le'Veon Bell, who became one of the best players in the NFL with his ability to both run and catch the ball. The Steelers' other major offensive star under Tomlin was wide receiver Antonio Brown.

Brown was the steal of the 2010 draft. Pittsburgh got him in the sixth round, out of seven rounds total. Many players taken that low never play in the NFL. But Brown became one of the best receivers in Steelers history. He had his first 1,000-yard receiving season in 2011. From 2013 to 2018, Brown posted at least 1,200 receiving yards each season. That included leading all of the NFL in 2014 and 2017. By the end of the 2018 season, Brown was fewer than 1,000 yards behind Ward for most receiving yards in team history.

TROY POLAMALU

It was often hard to read Troy Polamalu's name on his jersey. But you would never mistake him for someone else. One reason was the long black hair that covered his name. Another reason was his hard hits. Polamalu was a first-round draft pick in 2003. The safety made eight Pro Bowls in his career and won NFL Defensive Player of the Year in 2010. He made only 32 career interceptions, but many were spectacular. One of his most memorable was in the 2008 AFC Championship Game. Polamalu picked off Joe Flacco and returned it 40 yards for a touchdown that sent the Steelers to the Super Bowl. Polamalu played his entire career in Pittsburgh and retired in 2015.

JuJu Smith-Schuster, *left*, had just turned 22 when he was voted to the Pro Bowl in 2018.

And of course, the Steelers had a strong defense. Linebacker James Harrison, safety Troy Polamalu, and defensive end Cameron Heyward were some standout players under Tomlin.

The Steelers gave up the fewest points in the NFL in 2008, 2010, and 2011.

But despite great players, the Steelers struggled to replicate their Super Bowl success. After losing to the Green Bay Packers in Super Bowl XLV, Pittsburgh only advanced as far as the 2016 AFC Championship Game over the next eight seasons.

Even though the Steelers weren't winning championships, they were never far off. Tomlin had never had a losing season. His teams made the playoffs eight times in his first 12 years in Pittsburgh. And with budding superstars such as wide receiver JuJu Smith-Schuster and pass-rushing specialist T. J. Watt providing hope, the future looked bright. Pittsburgh has shown throughout its history that it should never be counted out for long.

STRONG SUPPORT

"Steeler Nation" is the nickname given to Steelers fans, who, as a group, have a reputation of being as dedicated as any in American professional sports. Legendary NFL films narrator John Facenda is credited as the first to use the term, in the 1970s. Pittsburgh fans are known for showing up in other cities in such large numbers that some other NFL teams have taken steps to limit ticket sales to fans from the Pittsburgh area.

TIMELINE

Art Rooney forms an NFL franchise in Pittsburgh and names it the Pirates.

The Pittsburgh Pirates football team is renamed the Steelers.

Due to a player shortage during World War II, the Steelers and the Philadelphia Eagles combine for one season as the Phil-Pitt Steagles.

The Steelers and the Chicago Cardinals combine for one season as the Chi/Pitt Cards/Steelers.

The Steelers play in their first playoff game, losing 21–0 to the Eagles.

1933

1940

1943

1944

1947

Chuck Noll is hired as head coach of the Steelers.

The Steelers win a playoff game for the first time with the help of Franco Harris's "Immaculate Reception," beating the Oakland Raiders 13–7.

The Steelers draft future Hall of Famers Lynn Swann, Jack Lambert, John Stallworth, and Mike Webster.

Pittsburgh defeats the Minnesota Vikings 16–6 in Super Bowl IX on January 12.

The Steelers repeat as Super Bowl champions with a 21–17 victory over the Dallas Cowboys on January 18.

1969

1972

1974

1975

1976

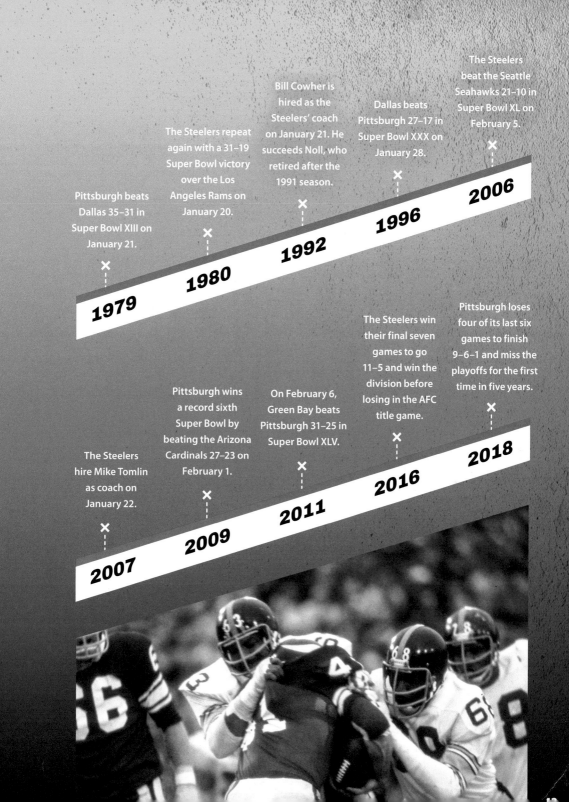

Pittsburgh beats Dallas 35–31 in Super Bowl XIII on January 21.

1979

The Steelers repeat again with a 31–19 Super Bowl victory over the Los Angeles Rams on January 20.

1980

Bill Cowher is hired as the Steelers' coach on January 21. He succeeds Noll, who retired after the 1991 season.

1992

Dallas beats Pittsburgh 27–17 in Super Bowl XXX on January 28.

1996

The Steelers beat the Seattle Seahawks 21–10 in Super Bowl XL on February 5.

2006

The Steelers hire Mike Tomlin as coach on January 22.

2007

Pittsburgh wins a record sixth Super Bowl by beating the Arizona Cardinals 27–23 on February 1.

2009

On February 6, Green Bay beats Pittsburgh 31–25 in Super Bowl XLV.

2011

The Steelers win their final seven games to go 11–5 and win the division before losing in the AFC title game.

2016

Pittsburgh loses four of its last six games to finish 9–6–1 and miss the playoffs for the first time in five years.

2018

QUICK STATS

FRANCHISE HISTORY

Pittsburgh Pirates (1933–40)
Pittsburgh Steelers (1941–42)
Phil-Pitt Steagles (1943)
Chi/Pitt Cards/Steelers (1944)
Pittsburgh Steelers (1945–)

SUPER BOWLS
(wins in bold)

1974 (IX), **1975 (X)**, **1978 (XIII)**,
1979 (XIV), 1995 (XXX), **2005 (XL)**,
2008 (XLIII), 2010 (XLV)

NFL CHAMPIONSHIP GAMES *(1933–69)*

AFC CHAMPIONSHIP GAMES *(since 1970 AFL-NFL merger)*

1972, 1974, 1975, 1976, 1978, 1979,
1984, 1994, 1995, 1997, 2001, 2004,
2005, 2008, 2010, 2016

KEY COACHES

Bill Cowher (1992–2006):
   149–90–1, 12–9 (playoffs)
Chuck Noll (1969–91): 193–148–1,

KEY PLAYERS
(position, seasons with team)

Jerome Bettis (RB, 1996–2005)
Mel Blount (CB, 1970–83)
Terry Bradshaw (QB, 1970–83)
Antonio Brown (WR, 2010–)
"Mean" Joe Greene (DT, 1969–81)
Jack Ham (LB, 1971–82)
Franco Harris (RB, 1972–83)
John Henry Johnson (RB, 1960–65)
Jack Lambert (MLB, 1974–84)
Troy Polamalu (S, 2003–14)
Ben Roethlisberger (QB, 2004–)
John Stallworth (WR, 1974–87)
Ernie Stautner (G/DL, 1950–63)
Lynn Swann (WR, 1974–82)
Mike Webster (C, 1974–88)
Rod Woodson (DB, 1987–96)

HOME FIELDS

Heinz Field (2001–)
Three Rivers Stadium (1970–2000)
Pitt Stadium (1964–69)
Forbes Field and Pitt Stadium
   (1958–63)
Forbes Field (1933–57)

* All statistics through 2018 season

QUOTES AND ANECDOTES

Steelers broadcaster Myron Cope created the Terrible Towel in 1975. The yellow terrycloth towels remain a hot item among Pittsburgh fans, particularly when the team is in one of its Super Bowl runs. Cope turned over the trademark of the $7 towels to the Allegheny Valley School in 1996. The school is a network of campuses and group homes that cares for people with severe intellectual and developmental disabilities. The Allegheny Valley School receives almost all proceeds from the towels. Cope's son Danny is among those who have been cared for by the Allegheny Valley School.

"I believe the game is designed to reward the ones who hit the hardest. If you can't take it, you shouldn't play."

> —Jack Lambert, middle linebacker on the Steelers' Steel Curtain defenses of
> the 1970s

Bill Dudley led the NFL in rushing as a rookie in 1942 while also leading the team in passing. Dudley served in the Army Air Corps in World War II, then returned to the Steelers in 1945. He became the NFL's Most Valuable Player in 1946 when he led the league in rushing, punt returns, and interceptions.

The most distinctive feature of the Steelers' home of Heinz Field is the dual ketchup bottles atop the scoreboard. Each one is an exact replica of a real Heinz ketchup bottle. The bottles are 35 feet tall (11 m) and weigh 8,000 pounds (3,629 kg), but are made of fiberglass, not real glass. If the bottles were real, they would hold 1.66 million ounces (49.1 million mL) of ketchup.

The Steelers' helmet logo is based on the Steelmark logo for the steel industry. The stars on the logo represent the three ingredients of steel. The yellow one stands for coal, orange means iron ore, and blue means scrap steel. The logo has been on Pittsburgh helmets since 1962.

GLOSSARY

contender
A person or team that has a good chance at winning a championship.

contract
An agreement to play for a certain team.

draft
A system that allows teams to acquire new players coming into a league.

dual threat
Very good at two different skills, such as running and receiving.

franchise
A sports organization, including the top-level team and all minor league affiliates.

franchise quarterback
A quarterback who leads a team for a number of years.

merge
Join with another to create something new, such as a company, a team, or a league.

momentum
The sense that a team is playing well and will be difficult to stop.

Pro Bowl
The NFL's all-star game, in which the best players in the league compete.

retire
To end one's career.

rookie
A professional athlete in his or her first year of competition.

sack
A tackle of the quarterback behind the line of scrimmage before he can pass the ball.

MORE INFORMATION

BOOKS

Cohn, Nate. *Pittsburgh Steelers*. New York: AV2 by Weigl, 2018.

Graves, Will. *Pittsburgh Steelers*. Minneapolis, MN: Abdo Publishing, 2017.

Wilner, Barry. *Total Football*. Minneapolis, MN: Abdo Publishing, 2017.

ONLINE RESOURCES

Booklinks
NONFICTION NETWORK
FREE! ONLINE NONFICTION RESOURCES

To learn more about the Pittsburgh Steelers, visit **abdobooklinks.com** or scan this QR code. These links are routinely monitored and updated to provide the most current information available.

PLACE TO VISIT

Pro Football Hall of Fame
2121 George Halas Dr. NW
Canton, OH 44708
330–456–8207
profootballhof.com

This hall of fame and museum highlights the greatest players and moments in the history of the NFL. Those affiliated with the Steelers who are enshrined include Jerome Bettis and Terry Bradshaw.

INDEX

ABOUT THE AUTHOR

William Meier has worked as an author and editor in the publishing industry for more than 25 years. He resides in St. Louis, Missouri, with his wife and their poodle, Macy.